IMMATURE RHYMES

FOR

IMMATURE PEOPLE

RODERICK LOWBROW

Immature Rhymes for Immature People

ISBN 13: 978-0-9909010-4-4
1st Edition
Printed in the USA

RED
CROWN
publishing

I can burp the alphabet
Can burp from A to Z
I can burp it out in sequence
I can burp it randomly
I burp when I say W
I burp when I say T
I burp at K L M or O
I also burp at D
I burp them out of order
I burp R and then burp G
A burp at H, some more at C
Y, X, U and V
E deserves a special burp
As does S and so does P
I can also burp them back to front
So I burps before B
I burp F and J and Q
And then I'm burping N
When there's no more letters
I burp the alphabet again

Peeing your name in the snow
Is a fun thing to do
And with practice you'll only get
better
But some names are too long
And with limited pee
You'll only get to the nineth letter

Try not to laugh when you're
farting
People will know when you do
If someone farts and you are
still
laughing
They will always assume it was
you

Sorry for cropdusting grandma
It was just an honest mistake
I let one rip walking before her
And left a big fart in my wake

Never eat the yellow snow
It's not like lemon ice
There is no fruit flavor at all
In fact it won't taste nice

Peeing on the urinal cake
Is my favorite thing to do
My pee has started yellow
By the end it's colored blue

Farting in the bath tub gives me
bubbles
Makes me feel like I am sitting in
a spa
While a jacuzzi can blow bubbles
out for hours
My farting doesn't get me very far

I'm peeing in the
bathroom
I'm peeing on the floor
I'm peeing on the
windows
I'm peeing on the door
And when my
bladders empty
That's the moment I
know when
To go and drink more
water
So that I can pee
again

Muffle a fart in the
cushions
Be careful so no one can
hear
It might make the cushion
quite stinky
So don't hold it up to your
ear

Tiny boogers up nose make me
crazy
Tiny boogers make me feel like
I'm insane
But I should not use a pencil to
pick them
Cause there's a chance that it
could stab me in the brain

It's not proper to fart out in public
It's a socially bad thing to do
Unless nobody hears when you do it
And no one can blame it on you

A fart in car is disgusting
Because everyone's locked inside
You must quickly lower the window
It's smelling like something has died

There's a fart in my
butt that I've gotta get
out of my butt
There's a fart in my
butt that I've gotta get
out of my butt
There's a fart in my
butt, but I can't get it
out
So I push and I
squeeze and I scream
and I shout
There's a fart in my
butt that I've gotta get
out of my butt

Your nose hairs are waving at me
I can see them quite clearly from
here
They're not just the only hairs
waving
You've also got hair in your ear

That puddle was there
when I got here
I did not just pee on the
floor
But the puddle I think could
be bigger
So I decided to pee on it
more

I've got a tiny little fart stuck in
my butt hole
I can feel it start to bubble in my
guts
I've got a tiny little first stuck my
butt hole
And it kinda makes me feel I'm
going nuts

There's broccoli for dinner
in ten
I count down the minutes to
when
Three hours after
Through giggles and
laughter
I'm burping up broccoli
again

Even the Queen of England farts
So believe me when I tell
That when she sits upon her throne
She can leave a royal smell

Do you like it when your farts are really smelly?
Do you like it when your farts clear out the room?
Do you like it when you're farting really quiet
Or maybe when they come out with a boom?

My parents just bought me
new sneakers
The leather was shiney and
white
But I slipped over in dog
poo
Now there is no white in
sight

A fart is a secret
weapon
One that is easy to hide
But once you have
chosen to use it
People will think that
they've died

A fart pops out to say
hello
And as quick as it
arrives
It leaves a stinky
cloud of fumes
To ruin people's lives

I peed on my shoe in the bathroom
Now it's all chilly and wet
My sock is clammy and stinky
I don't know how much worse it
could get

My farts don't smell like
ice cream
That would be quite absurd
'cuz if they smelled like ice
cream
Would ice cream smell like
turd?

Farts is a five letter word
Like comet, or money, or
laugh
But the difference with
money and farting
Is dollars will not make you
barf

I fart in the morning
And one more time at
night
I fart again at lunch
time
And at evening while
there's light
And when I crawl
beneath the covers
Once my day is at an
close
I save my biggest fart
of all
To terrorize my nose

If I burp right after eating
It's my way of saying yum
And if choose to fart instead
It's a thank you from my bum

While a fart on my own makes me giggle
If others do hear then I blush
I'm horrified someone has heard it
To the exit I head in a rush

Poopsie McGee is a
farting machine
His farts are
reknowned over town
But his continuous
farting brings him
one small
concern
His undies are
frequently brown

People fart around
the world
It's more common
than you think
Everybody living on
the planet
Has a moment where
they stink

Today I just heard a rumor
That even the famous folk
fart
From actors, musicians,
performers
And people who like to paint
art
So take just a small bit of
comfort
If you're Beyonce, Hemsworth
or just Philip
That no matter what's in your
bank acoount
That we all need to just let
one rip

Did you know your
grandma farts?
I promise you it's true
While she may seem sweet and
innocent
She can rip as good as you

They may start out small and
quiet
With a toot or softer squeaks
But eighteen seconds later
Something really reeks

So next time when you hug
her
And you squeeze with all your
heart
Make sure you pay attention
As you may hear grandma fart

Always blame children for
farting
When nobody hears that it's
you
Cause grown ups will always
blame children
Whenever they are smelling
poo

One fart
Two fart
Soft fart

LOUD FART

To burp after eating's good
manners
It means that your cooking is
great
I get to taste it one more time
Even though I cleaned off my
plate

Don't cut toe nails in the
kitchen
It will always put mom in a
mood
Some may end up on the
counters
While others may land in
your food

Try not to fart when you're
swimming
When others are trying to
play
People will know that you did
it
The bubbles will give you
away

Ricky had a little fart
It was quite nauesating
He would not stop while sat
in school
His friends found it
frustrating

A fart in your face
means I love you
It's my way that I
show you I care
Because if I found
you
annoying
I wouldn't leave any
fart there

There's been over forty
presidents
In the whole U.S of A
And I promise you sincerely
They all fart everyday

While sitting in the
Whitehouse
At the Oval Office table
They lift a cheek and
squeeze one out
Whenever they are able

Tiny bubbles in the bathtub means
you're farting
Tiny bubbles in the bathtub means
there's gas
Tiny bubbles make me giggle in
amusement
So enjoy the tiny bubbles while
they last

Your mom and your dad have both
farted

Even if they say that's a lie

The rumor is mom's are quite stinky

Just one whiff and you'll start to cry

Bobby is famous for
farting
He has farted non
stop for a year
He started in June
Through sun and
through moon
It's now May and his
farts are still here

My finger went through the toilet
paper
While I was wiping my butt dry
The paper tore through in an
instant
And now I am starting to cry

I'm sorry I peed on the floor
I thought I was aiming just right
But I noticed a puddle was spreading
I should have just turned on the
light

Breaking wind and cutting
cheese
Are both ways to say fart
A Bronx cheer, trump and
ringbark
Or maybe raspberry tart
But it doesn't matter which
you use
To describe the ways you
smell
It's only about how bad it
stinks
It's how you know that you've
done well

Leaving the toilet seat up
Is a most
unforgivable crime
For someone to put it down
for you
Is a ridiculous waste of
their time

Because the effort for
someone to close it
Takes at most just a second
or two
So if they cannot be
bothered
They're just as lazy as you

If you're gassy and you
know it try to fart!
If you're gassy and you
know it try to fart!
If you're gassy and you
know it clench your
cheeks get set to blow
it
If you're gassy and you
know it try to fart!

Eggy farts are quite
disgusting
Of all the farts I
think they are the
worst
So if you smell an
eggy fart
Make sure you get
out first

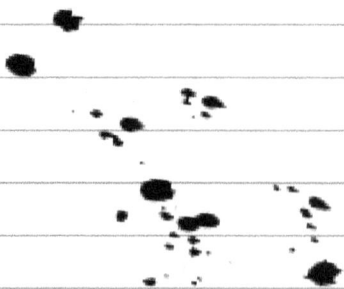

I fart when I
sneeze and I giggle
I fart when I cough
and I cheer
I fart when I yawn
When I jump on
the lawn
I fart singing
happy new year

Bobby squeaked a
little fart
One that smelled
disgusting
It's not the worst
part of it all
He did it while
cropdusting

I have to do the pee pee
dance
But the line is moving
slow
The bathroom wait is far
to long
And I really need to go

My farting is worse after
broccoli
I promise that this is true
So if you've been feeding
me broccoli
Don't be surprised when I'm
farting on you

The best way to
say thank you for
food
Is by belching and
or by tooting
It's complimentary
to the chef
When the air you
start polluting

Farting in the afternoon
Is how I spend my day
If you see me giggling
You should just run away

Farting is healthy
Farting is fun
If you hear my fart coming
You might want to run

Is it rude if I burp after
eating?
Is it rude if I let out a fart?
The air has come in while
enjoying the food
But there are only two ways
to depart

The louder the burp
The bigger the yell
The louder the fart
The grosser the smell

Something is
stewing
I feel a fart
brewing
Be careful when
starting to sniff
As the smell grows
It may waft up
your nose
And you may get a
bit of a whiff

Cropdusting is specialized
farting
That takes skill and
practice to do
The trick is for you to keep
moving
And leaving the fart behind
you

Can you smell what I smell?
It's really, really gross
It smells like cheese and rotten
eggs
Or something very close

An apple a day keeps
the doctor away
But farting can make
you feel well
And farting a day is
cheaper than apples
Except for the terrible
smell

Eenie Meenie Minie Mo
Sorry I just farted
I did not want to take the blame
So I quickly departed

Stinky, stinky little fart
You came out quick
Slow to depart
You linger in the room
So long
Started weak and ended
strong

I see you sniff the air
It is my fart you smell
I will never say it's mine
I swear I'll never tell

I have a confession to
make
My stomach has
started to ache
I thought it was
sneeking
My farts are now
reeking
A bean burrito was a
mistake

Try no to fart in the
kitchen
While mother is getting
things done
If she smells that you've
been stinking
Pack up your things and
then run

Billy's been farting all
day and all night
It's driving his parents
quite mad
They could forgive the
noise and laughs
But they hated the farts
smelled so bad

Jenny was a
lovely girl
Intelligent and
classy
But she loved to
burp and do things
gross
And was
frequently quite
gassy

I was farting at
the mall the other
day
Cropdusting all the
people out to play
I was farting and
was shopping
While a cloud of
gas was dropping
And the smell it
helped to get them
out the way

Farts are gross and farts
are smelly
They are often quite
appalling
But they always make
bystanders laugh
Each time your butt is
calling

It's not proper to fart at
the grocery store
It's where people like to
go and buy their food
They don't like to smell
poop when they're
shopping
It can put them in a very
grumpy mood

It's 7:00 a.m. and my alarm
clock is ringing
My bed I don't want to
depart
The room it falls silent as
my face starts to grin
And I let out an earth
shaking fart

It is not cool to fart in
school
Because classmates will
all tease
So do it where no one is
found
And you'll fart as you
please

I like to eat my vegetables
I eat them every night
Like cabbage, beans and brussel sprouts
And broccoli tastes just right
But when my dinner's settled
And a rumbling is just starting
The veggies give me massive gas
And I spend ninety minutes farting

Sorry for my belching
It wasn't very smart,
But if it left the other end
It would've been a fart

The rumbling deep inside
of me
Is singing songs within my
gut
It's just my tummy's
symphony
That plays music from my
butt

Oh what a wonderful
morning
Oh what a wonderful
day
I just let a juicy big
fart out
It's just my butt's way
to say hey

A burp is just a northern
breeze
That's rushing to depart
But when it takes a
southern turn
It changes to a fart

I may have just farted
while lying in bed
It smells so bad under the
sheet
I couldn't believe that smell
came out of me
But I can't tell if it's fart or
my feet

Toilet paper you are so
fantastic
You are soft and very
gentle on our butts
I'm glad you're made of
paper not of plastic
And do not give us nasty
paper cuts

Everyone eats boogers
Be it parent, child or
teacher
Doctors, lawyers,
nurses too
And probably the
preacher
From fireman to bus
drivers
Be it cop or astronaut
But the trick to
eating boogers
Is to try not to get
caught

As I sit and ponder
life
My tummy started
falling
My thoughts of peace
escape me
As my farts they smell
appalling

The new toilet roll is so
perfect and white
It makes it so poop doesn't
linger
I have to be careful when
wiping too hard
That poop doesn't get on
my finger

I'm cutting the cheese with
the greatest of ease
I can fart when I'm not
really trying
But if I focus real hard and
put in the effort
I make it smell like
something is dying

Life is like a fart that blows
in the wind
Here right now and then
gone in a blink
A day is like a fart that
wafts up your nose
Some have no scent while
others just stink

If someone hears me fart I
blame the doggie
I'm someone hears me me
fart I blame the pet
If someone hears me fart
I'll pretend it was not me
I'll blame the pup until we
all forget

I've recently ran out of
tp
In the cabinet I
thought I had some
But it turns out the
cabinet's empty
There's nothing to use
on my bum

I do love to fart when I'm walking
It makes me feel lighter than air
Sometimes there's people around me
And sometimes nobody is there

Hush little baby don't you cry
That smell I'll blame on you, not I
All you do is stink and poo
That's why it's easy to blame you

A fart can make you queezy
A fart can make you sick
And if that fart came out of
you
You'd better duck out quick

Any time I'm feeling
down
I know what makes me
glad
I can make a smile come
from a frown
With a fart that smells
so bad

There's nothing more
enjoyable than farting
There's nothing that's
more fun than
passing gas
You can sing, or
throw a ball
Paint a picture on a
wall
But give up farting?
No I think I'll pass

Humpty Dumpty sat on a
wall
From his perch he then
quickly departed
He hit the ground hard and
he shattered tp pieces
All because poor Humpty
farted

I was sitting there in
silence
It was just me on my own
Suddenly I heard a sound
The massive fart that I'd
just blown

The flaming bag of
poo
Is sitting on your
porch
Please consider this
rhyme my admission
The flaming bag of
poo has no flames at
all
Because I carried
nothing for ignition

I just ripped the biggest
fart the world has ever
heard
Every living thing could
hear it
From a rhino to a bird

When the sound has
settled
And the world starts
re-adjusting
That's the time the stink
creeps in
It's really quite
disgusting

They say that he who smelled it dealt it
But I don't think that is fair
You can't be blamed for someone's fart
That they put in the air
So if you're pointing fingers
To give someone else the blame
They may just fart and point at you
So you can share their shame

A fart is how your butt
says hi
It's just being polite
Because if it ignored
you
That would not be right
So the next time you
hear someone fart
Please don't think them
crude
It's just their butt with
manners
To ignore you would be
rude

I squeeze my cheeks and
clench my butt
A giant fart is brewing
But I notice you have got
some food
And you just started
chewing
I try my best to keep it in
And not to act repulsive
But I lift my leg and fart
out loud
Because I am impulsive

Have you ever sneezed so
hard
That a boogers flew out of
your nose
That a bubble of snot
sprayed all over your face
And slime got all over your
clothes

You should never put a
booger in a toaster
Because there is a change
it could ignite
And then you have toaster
full of boogers
And in future toast will
never taste quite right

One fart means yes
Two farts mean no
If you asked me if I
farted
One fart will tell you
so

There's a baby in the
bedroom making stinkies
Its diaper is a smelly awful
mess
So now's the best time for
you to be farting
And if someone says "who
farted" don't confess

I'm farting out in public
I'm farting in the car
I'm farting in the library
I'm farting near and far
And when there's
nowhere else go
And nowhere I can roam
I turn around and head
on back
So I can fart at home

Why is it that boogers
are tasty?
Why is it that boogers
taste great?
I can promise you'd
wouldn't eat boogers
If they were served
on a plate

Veronica's farts were out
of this world
Some people call them
amazing
She'd stand out at night
with her head lifted high
Was she farting or
simply stargazing?

Now my rhymes are
at an end
It's time I must
depart
But I'd never dream
to stop this book
Without a massive

FART!!

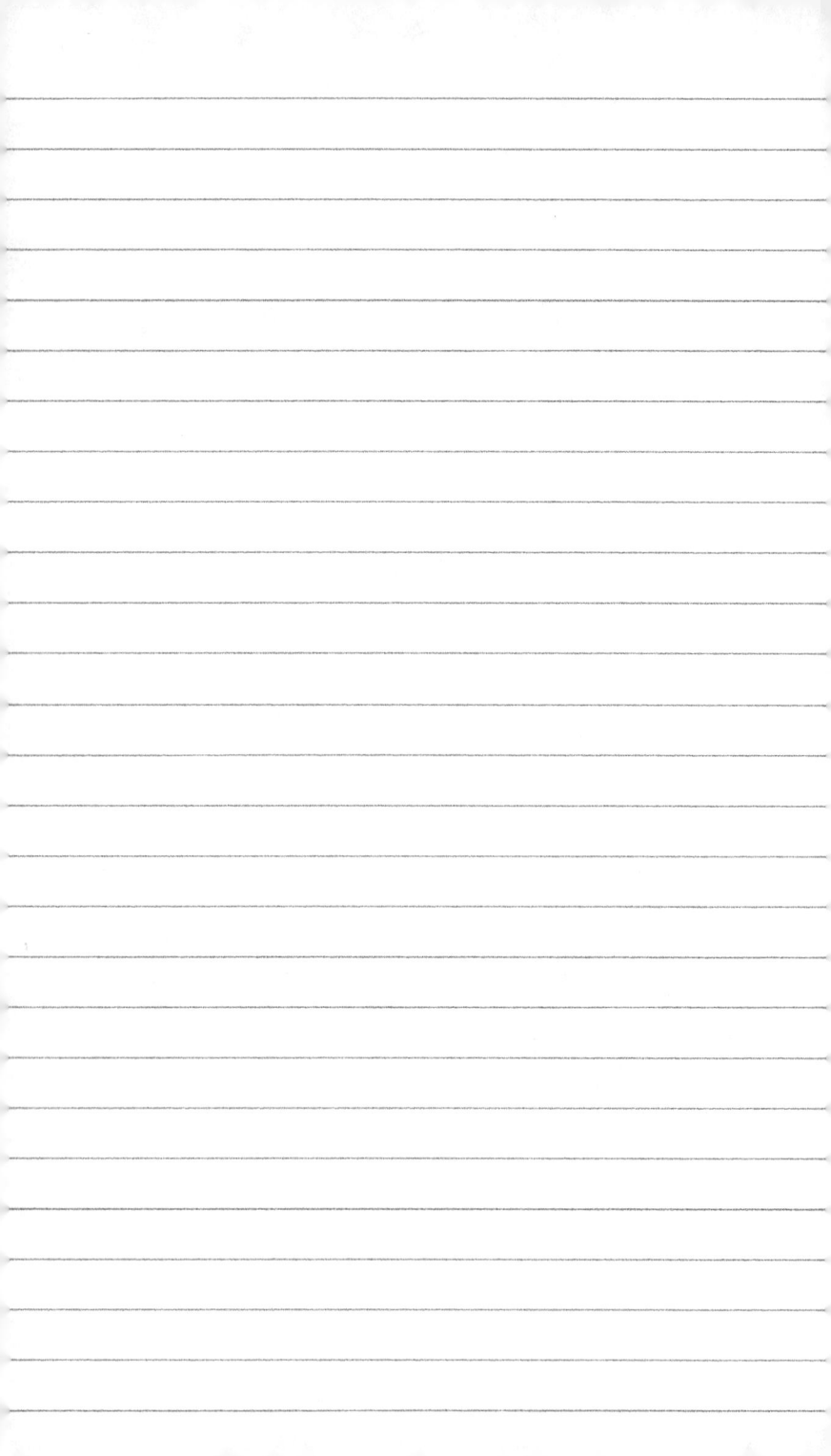

CREATE YOUR OWN FART AND BURP RHYMES!

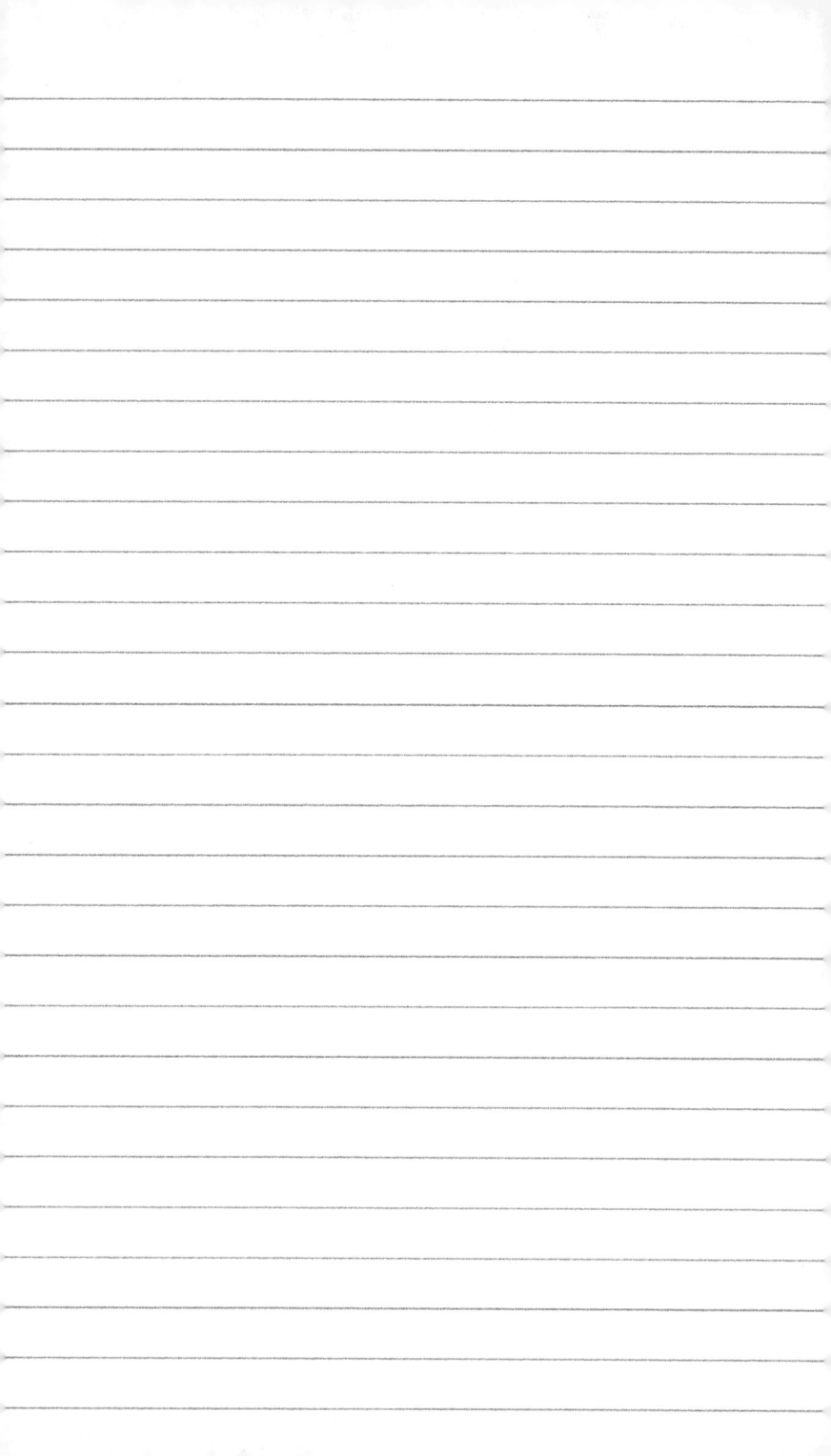